Pat Winslow
Skin & Dust

To Barbara

Kind regards

Pat 2005.

i

First published 2004
by:
Blinking Eye Publishing
North Shields
NE1 7RU

ISBN: 0-9549036-0-9

www.blinking-eye.co.uk
for further information about Blinking Eye Publishing
please visit our website
or write to the above address.

Blinking Eye Publishing acknowledges
the financial assistance of The Northern Arts Council (England).

Cover photography by Adam Lawrenson,
Forrest Hall.
Printed in Great Britain:
thenewprinthouse Ltd. North Shields

Acknowledgements

Back Room Poets; Barnet Borough Arts Council Poetry Anthology;
Brando's Hat; the Housman Society; the Interpreter's House; Iota;
the Jumping Cat
(hometown.aol.co.uk/jumpcatrod/myhomepage/writing.html);
Kent and Sussex Poetry Society; Leviathan Quarterly; Magma;
Obsessed With Pipework; the Poetry Café; Poetry News; PROP;
Ragged Raven Press; Rain Dog; the Reader; the Rialto;
Salford Women Writers; Stand; the Tram Arts Project, Salford.

The Cave was commissioned by LIME (www.limeart.org)

Photograph on back cover: Helen Kitchen

CONTENTS

Rise

Marvellous how the house builds itself
and knocks itself into shape,
how water pipes chug into place
and snug close behind the cupboards.

The arthritic stairs rear up,
creaking and groaning.
Boards slat flatways on top of risers
all the way to the attic.

Doors stand tall. Each room defines itself.
Cracks and bumps slot themselves in.
The plaster goes on layer by layer.
Skirts and architraves grip the walls.

Carpet rods nail themselves down.
Wallpaper sheets butt up to each other.
Paint slaps itself on, sockets dig themselves in
and cables branch out like veins.

Clever how time asserts itself before
the clock arrives on the bedside table.
And now comes colour. It's like those films
where monochrome past becomes full-blown Fuji.

It's a bleeding in, a bulking up.
And here's me last of all,
shaping myself in bed, pulling my skin on,
feeling it snub my fingers and toes. Careful.

Here are my feet and here's my face, my tongue,
the arch of my back, my fists, my mouth,
the whole of me, stretching and reaching out
and drawing back the curtains.

The Dry Season

It didn't take long for the grass to go brown,
for the rust to make the hinges seize up altogether.
It didn't take long for the unwanted things to take over.

I saw their faces pressed close behind the shed.
The leaves of the lilac were hanging like rags.
Everything was sap-sticky and scratched by dust.

They won't come out. They'll stay for weeks if they have to,
amongst the spiders, between the plant pots,
staring, listening, waiting for a break in the weather.

The Balaclava

All winter she wore it like a collapsed smile.
Lopsided, from eyebrow to jowl, a flap of loose skin.
Pedicle head. A pea in a turquoise pod.

If she turned left, she disappeared inside it.
If she turned right, it followed her round.

They were mornings to see your breath in.
A local tarn shone like polished metal.
There were ice-runs in the streets.

We woke to whatever the night had knitted together:
white-sleeved trees, icicles under the bridge.

In second gear up Wrynose Pass,
she said one false slip and we'd be over the edge.
The melodrama in those eyes.

The crash and tumble, flailing doors, bags, gloves, scarf,
tyres thumping, panels, bumpers sheering off.

Two spider's webs of broken glass and our heads
were jammed up tight, hers, a soft blur of blue wool,
kingfisher in the creeping fog of late afternoon.

Then, police lights, men in navy, heavy boots. The balaclava
slurred sideways, as if to say I told you so, a plain-purl smirk.

The Place That People Made

You tread a corrugated iron path,
leave rusty footprints in the grass.

Think tetanus, think jagged wounds
stitched shut with nylon thread.

But carry on, because
this is where the safe place is.

Breezeblocks and an asbestos roof,
a plastic sheet held down by stones.

Jungle light fills the space.
Garden chairs face inwards.

There's a galvanised bin for a fire,
an ashtray kept empty and clean.

Curtains add a kitchen touch.
Nets and a strip of blind conceal

the dark place at the back.
Serious business happens there.

A table and a bed of carpet samples
testify to that.

The smell is secret and earthy.
WE KNOW it says on the wall.

Evenings watching rain
drip on the nettles outside.

The smell of weed
comes thick and sweet.

Anything can happen here.
It probably does.

There's always the ropeway
to guide you to the river.

There go the ducks.
There goes the certainty of water.

And there, twinkling, hushing,
goes the world in all its distance.

George's Pike

George paints a canal straight down the middle
of two tables we've set for stories – newspapers
and bonnets and royal souvenirs are forgotten.

The fisherman's basket did it, the flies and reel,
30 foot's pushing it, I say. No, he tells me.
It's correct. No one knows what's down there.

Oliver's boys hurl stones at a bargee going past.
They draw words as colourful as robbed fruit.
A heron stands like a schoolmaster among the reeds.

The water shoves at the mud. All this churning.
There are damselflies and dabchicks, moorhens, coots.
A thin film of diesel reflects a dragonfly's wings.

In the evening mist, girls walk by, arm in arm.
They glad eye a boy with a dog – it's important to have
the right sort of dog – but he's too shy to talk.

He just keeps walking, wishes he'd been cheekier,
had the nerve of the rowdies. Now they're gone
and the canal is wading into the night.

A horse comes towing a rope, head down, muscles taut.
A stone rolls over the edge. I hear it plop,
see George's pike watching our shadows, waiting.

Armistice Day, 2003

The fog is the wartime milk
my mother talked about.

It's also the cotton wool tread of a tank
rolling over our heads, burying us in sleep.

Birds cluster like black fruit
in the dripping silence.

Two men are chiselling wood
and hammering nails.

Colours bundle close to the house –
hedges are the last line of resistance,

unless you count the continuous
which is as brave as lipstick today.

It's not hard to imagine the lost field
sharing the fate of others –

stumps of trees like stalagmites,
tobacco tins heeled into the mud

with spent ammunition
and all the rest.

What sticks in the mind
is the rescued man

jabbering in the boat,
his hands strangely neat in his lap.

Did they feel light suddenly,
or were they heavy as history?

Outside, the old men
have done what they came to do.

The builders are on a tea break
and the birds have gone.

The fog is stealing everything.
You could forget there was a rest of the world.

You could forget everything but for the planes
heaving out of Brize Norton.

The History Lesson

Memories are never still. Sometimes they flutter
like hands and come to rest between two plates.
You can drop your knife and fork amongst them
and they'll flit and settle somewhere else.

Should the past accumulate like dust,
the slightest movement will whisk it away.
A face might turn into another face or slip
inside your own, and whose then do you trust?

Even mirrors will lose their meanings.
I saw a woman speaking to herself once.
Her fingers pressed against the glass to touch her hair.
Sometimes there's no way back to the present.

Today's memories are huge and sad,
heaving into chairs and almost breaking them.
They've come a long way to be here
and seem more corporeal than their owners.

We pack them up like parcels and take them home.
Tomorrow, something new will catch the eye.
Something like a seed of mercury will glint
and call others to itself. We'll tread more carefully.

We'll look down and find our own feet unsteady.
We'll look up to find that someone else is listening.

Last Supper

That night, at ten o'clock, she began eating herself.
No one stopped her – as if we ever could.
She hooked her legs like a coat hanger
beneath her chin, started on her toes
and worked her way upwards.
She seemed to take forever,
sucking and swallowing.
Her silvery abdomen
ballooned outwards.
Twice she stopped
and stared at us
we thought.

We stood
in our doorways,
witnessed her hips
leaving, the glistening
moon of her belly as she
balanced it between her teeth.
She gagged and closed both eyes –
no room, surely – and forced it down.
Her arms slid like spaghetti. Shoulders,
thorax, neck. She sipped the last of her spine.
She turned herself inside out like a sock, left her lips
till last, then she ate her head, gulped once and disappeared.

Curzon's Foundling

'...the English traveller who visited Athos came across a man
who had been left as a foundling on the peninsula'

Try to imagine infinity. You can't
put doors on it, nail walls in place.
It's like God. It's also like nothing.
Saying 'nothing' gives it substance.

I've never seen a woman.
Don't ask me what that means.
Ask me what I know. Stone robes
is what I know. Byzantine gold.

And cracked skin – crimson lake,
a dab of china white, ochre, ultramarine.
Haloes are crescent moons that rise
like antlers from a ridge of bone.

I can imagine washing marble hair,
feel the blank weight of it rocking
in the sink before I buff it dry
and polish it with cloth.

In certain lights – a candle in a cup –
eyes which look heavenwards or down
will stare at me. Briefly. I don't spend
too much time in contemplation.

It does no good to spread oneself
along her arms and legs, to match
her palms with mine or cover her heart
with my own soft beating feathers.

That's how I feel. Like a bird
blown off course, clinging to air.
So small and white and fragile,
she could snap my bones.

Ordnance Survey

You wake up one morning to find that someone's
run a highlighter pen up the centre of your road.
In the old days it was all biro marks and bits of
dust, Ambre Solaire thumbprints that were hard to
get rid of. The waves have gone dog-eared. Time
to move on, you say. But you can't. There's the
kids and school. In any case, two black chevrons
block your way. They've been there since '52
when the man came to measure the hill. It's steep,
he told you. Very steep. His Ford Popular broke
down on a contour line. You had to tow him
down. He comes back sometimes. Fond
memories, he says. His is a precarious existence.
He lives on a fold eleven miles away. Every now
and then he falls off, loses all his friends. It takes
days to find them. He hasn't seen his wife for
seven years. She's on the other side, he says
bitterly. One day all of this will be sea, the
climatologists claim. You'll build a boat and go
from white to blue and darker blue again. You'll
find a grid line and follow it. 58 sounds good. 58
09. Turn south at 51. Just keep going.

Matthew

The room smells of milk, our backs are straight.
We're reciting *once five is five, two fives are ten.*

I love Mrs Dredge. Her ruler taps the numbers.
Nine fives are forty-five, ten fives are fifty.

The exercise book smells of cigarettes.
She's got fuzzy skin. Her hair is like feathers.

They make us drink milk from small glass bottles.
The gas fire flames are popping. *Once six is six.*

Andrew Bush has a bogey up his nose
like a big yellow balloon. *Two sixes.*

It blobs in and out when he speaks.
Twelve. He has a hanky he never uses.

Listen! I don't know how this happens,
that first slap and Matthew's ow of surprise,

but there's a second, a third, a fourth, a fifth.
Matthew's bottom wobbles like pink jelly.

The gas fire hisses between each crack.
Her hand is imprinted on his flesh.

Pull up your shorts.
The traffic outside the window throbs.

Her cheeks are gorged with blood.
Matthew's fingers tremble. His knees look scared.

Suddenly I love him. His face,
his mouth and nose, his wiry hair.

I can't stop looking. Matthew's eyes
are so big, so bovine and wet.

Legacy

In the silence she finds a lake of dust.
She wants to press her hand in it
and leave a perfect signature.

The even distribution of weight will tell you this –
she was small and middle aged,
she was careful and unmarried.

You won't have her name or the day she did it,
or what she was thinking about the dust.
If she had an opinion she took it with her.

That's all you'll know.
Except perhaps she didn't clean.
Couldn't, or she wouldn't.

MacMillan

His breath comes like city traffic.
Stop start buses, trembling taxis.
It's been gridlock since yesterday.
He won't last much longer.

Cancer's white. Sheets, sky,
the net curtains she pulls aside
to undo the window latch,
her plastic apron, rubber boots.

But not pain. Real pain's colourless.
Like the scouring agent they drip fed
into his veins. Much good that did.
Much good it ever does.

What colour's death?
Nobody talks about it.
It must be like walking backwards.
Which makes her think of its opposite.

Does it hurt to be born,
to tear yourself from nothing into being?
Does it hurt to enter your own skin?
It's a wonder we ever recover.

When his breathing stops,
his eyes go vivid blue with shock.
It's like he was never more alive than this.
She sees him leave. It happens a lot.

A bright flash, a phosphorescence
darting to the far corner of the room.
You feel their absence like a presence.
After a while that goes, too.

Sadness comes with little things.
Purses, wallets, reading glasses.
There's tenderness in the final wash,
the gift of water, the soft towel.

To be silent with the dead
is to be alone with yourself,
it's accepting that what matters most
was always going to be meaningless.

On Loan, Christ Church Picture Gallery

Auden,
book sized,
behind glass.

The rake of his head,
the overturned boat
of his hair sliding sidelong.

Monumental, slabbed.
Here's an edifice of a face
that's all pockets and pouches,

eyes like
slit-mouthed
mail sacks.

He's cavernous,
a cathedral of a man.
His fissured forehead is a cliff.

Teethmarks pock his lower lip.
A thick cigarette balances between
his thumb and forefinger.

His collar,
twin triangles of white,
sandwiches a loosely knotted tie.

You can almost smell
the nicotine stained words,
breathe in his years.

Hear him grunt and strain.
God, the concrete of him.
Such unassailable bulk.

Remembrance's Father Reads From the Bible

The coils of flax are swept up or else bagged.
The niddy-noddy is by the window.
It is bread and cheese today. No cooking.
Cold ham and a pie. He lifts both lamps,
fills them slowly and sets them in their trays.
Precisely. Evening weaves between our chairs
and gathers in the margins of the room.
He balances each lamp and takes a spill.
He lights them. One. Two. Twin flames mark his eyes.

The page rests like a world in his right hand.
He is finding the place with his finger.
'Remembrance. Elbows. Off the table, please.'
And feet, under it. My hands are folded.
Two birds in a lap. I can smell my blood,
metallic, warm. The whale oil smokes and curls.
Even now, I see it. The rimy weight
that was hauled in and carved up before us.
Corsets, combs, tallow, soap. Nothing wasted.

As the hour burns low, we grow less and less.
We are smudges and then we are nothing.
He takes all the light for himself. My blood
is unfurling like a ragged poppy
over the folded cloth. I do not hear.
The niddy-noddy is by the window.
The coils of flax are put to one side.
After, we shall have apples from the barrel.
Fat as summer. Crisp as tomorrow's frost.

Cutting up shirts for rags

opens a picture like a Quick Time file:
my mother trimming bacon rinds with scissors,

the blades' repetitive click as the strips of fat
fall loosely onto a china plate.

Another clip: the rubber bands she made
from washing-up gloves.

Wrists were best for tins, for keeping lids secure,
fingers for my Brooke Bond card collection.

I wonder if she remembers the pot of paint
she bought to smarten the bedroom furniture,

the dripping saved, the pears she cooked
and bottled for the winter months,

or how she used to layer lettuce leaves
between our sandwiches to keep them fresh,

the twist of salt that came with every egg –
things that ran through our lives

like a seam of soap saved and stuck
to the underside of each new bar?

She'd call me eccentric for keeping
the blanket knitted by TV light.

I have her wedding photo by my desk,
an Oxo tin, Quink bottles, Nivea, Vick.

It's a sort of holding hands
my habit of keeping her habits alive.

Perimeter

In the core of a white afternoon
everything coils or sleeps slitwise.

The world keeps its distance.
Heat bands change frequencies again and again.

It's the beginning of a long wait for nothing.
Mesquite pods tick. His rifle grows hot.

Stones. Skulls. Flesh. He's seen too much.
He's come to the vanishing point.

He watches. Listens to the wire's thin hum.
He licks his lips once and finds the salt.

Tastes the indifference.

The Visit

You know the picture will come again.
The back of the grey chair eases down.
You're horizontal. Just a scrape, he says.
You imagine the smile inside the mask,
try to guess what his breath smells like,
anything to stop the picture coming.

You knot your fingers loosely across the rise
and fall of your stomach. He's got the probe.
He's picking. He might say the numbers
of your teeth, call them out to the woman
rustling in the corner. The radio might be on.
A fly might be trapped against the window.

Nothing will stop it. It arrives when he sets
the scraper going, when the high whine
enters your head and you feel him pressing.
A photo, black and white, grainy, of a man
being lowered into a tank of icy water.
It's an experiment to see how long he'll live.

The dread, the numb terror of his stare.
You can't imagine him looking any other way.
He is that moment. That's how they did it.
Observing the reactions, not the man.
Poison gas, excisions, the panicky breath,
how a body, an organism, wants to live.

Other things you've read about are going on.
Batons, boots, hands tied back and hoisted up
between the shoulders, hoods, electrodes, stonings.
A judge will pass sentence and make it right.
A person will march another person to a place of death.
It's top shelf stuff. You shouldn't know about this.

Who's more degraded, the watcher or the watched?
He says rinse. The pink stuff tastes of Dentine.
Rinse and spit. The scouring foam is eddying
down the plughole. The white bowl glistens.
The rustling woman is handing you a tissue.
Quickly, now. Wipe your mouth, get up, walk out.

The Ferryman's Daughter

It was sunny when he pulled me out.

The men, I can't properly identify.
There were some. Several.
The one I remember pulled me out.

It was green underneath.

His hand reached down and grabbed me.
A sudden burst of light
like dammed breath exploding.

He had me by the ankles.

There were weeds on my feet, river mud.
The day turned green.
The ones on the grass never helped.

The man, I remember.

The man saw who pushed me,
who held me under.
Their clothes were green.

Perhaps.

Rings and prayers,
I don't remember.
There was an eel under a rock.

He's dead now, the man you could ask.

A man with hands like paddles.
There was a boat and a landing stage,
a house with smoke.

I forget his name.

A man reached in and got me.
A man breathed life in my mouth.
It goes black before that.

Before writing was used to keep historical records, a young child
was sometimes chosen to observe important proceedings then
thrown into a river. The memory of that event would be impressed
on the child and the record of the event maintained for the child's
lifetime

Afterworld

How are you now in your polished box?
What pared down perfection have you achieved?

Are your ribs like the struts of empty boats
lying side by side facing each other?

What smoothness, what sheen on the roof of your skull
might we find if we chose to look beneath the lid?

Here's the remarkable symmetry of your legs,
the cup and groove of every step you took,

the secret of your dancing, the way you sat,
snug as a mathematician's divider.

You're exactly where they laid you,
the red baseball cap, unbleached by all the summers,

only slightly disturbed by the falling away of flesh.
I'd forgotten they dressed you for the occasion.

Deliberately. Clothing makes you less real.
I prefer to think of the final state.

Bones are facts. They're indisputable.
It's best when we stop imagining

the voice on the phone, the creaking chair,
that the person at the bus stop might be you.

A Man Sits on the Roof of his Life

A man sits on a roof contemplating his feet.
There's a continuous line from the lower end
of his spine to the top of his head.
He is unbroken. He is hairless.

He's shining. His skin is the colour
of chimney pots. He's sitting whilst
small birds convene. He can hear
his own breathing. He finds this marvellous.

He has the weight of the night in his pockets
and the sky resting in the palm of each hand.
The day was white and insignificant
when he caught the bus.

He sang a song and no one heard it.
He sang it from the roof of his heart.
He watched the sun rise higher
and the ends of his feet grow lean.

He watched his life and knew it was full.
A man stands up and pitches himself forward.
There's a continuous line from the roof to the ground.
It is unbroken. He finds this marvellous.

Positive

You were waiting, listening to the shipping forecast.
The general synopsis at o-seven-hundred. The truck
was doing forty, forty-five. A pale boy with dreads
stepped out, a dog by his heels. The memory still stops you.

Low south Sweden one thousand and five.
You lit a cigarette and watched the crowd appear.
An ant was crawling on your knee, zigzagging across the scar.
The laburnum dripped yellow dust on your windscreen.

An ambulance arrived. Two women. Dykes.
You hadn't expected that. *Slowly east with little change.*
Thundery trough expected Thames to Humber.
The traffic lights changed and changed back.

When was the last time you saw that?
Two women. Some American cop show perhaps.
Not here. They lifted him up. You started the wipers,
thought of the barber's shop, the jar of barbicide.

They climbed in the back. Him with his stob of cold cigar,
jammed like a thumb, like an unsaid word. Gone out.
Why think of that now? Your father,
bending over your blond head in his tiny shop.

Viking. Your cut knee poking out from under the cape,
the metal comb flicking, his one towel does for all.
North Utsire, South Utsire. They shut the doors.
One dyke inside with him, the other behind the wheel.

They drove away. Left you chewing a perfect nail.
The dust was still falling. *Fair Isle, Faeroes, South East Iceland.*
The shipping forecast. That's how long it takes to see a doctor,
for a body to be strapped to a gurney and loaded up.

He got in. You threw your cigarette out of the window
and lit two more. One for him. His hands were shaking.
The dog was standing by the pool of blood.
No one would go near. Like that game - Last Look.

One glance and you've got it. Or catching the bride's bouquet.
You're next. Later, you turned around and drove back.
It hadn't moved. You picked it up and put it on his lap.
You took his hand. Tomorrow, you said. Tomorrow and tomorrow.

Michaelmas

Bicycles whisper in the yellow lanes
and candles tend our yearly absences.

The wind's on rubber legs today
down Trinity Street where the cloth boys meet.

The women are smoking French cigarettes.
They don't much care for interviews.

Owls fumble in the brickwork glory holes
of Gear Street and Tuppence Ha'penny Street.

Books climb the shelves to grow fat and old.
The bell keeps clapping out the years.

A brand new kettle boils in almost every room.
Soon it will be the season of toast and butter.

The moon unzips its laughter and slides
into the bottom of a white shaving bowl.

All the wrongs of unsung hands are shaking out the day.
The night's writing holds its awkward silence.

Later, it stupefies us by falling in tender barcodes.
See how it makes shiny hat wearers of us all.

Learning the Language of Buses

They arrived in the city of noise, overdressed
and lost, with their half-awake smiles.
For twelve hours the plane had been a void
between the moon and what they'd left behind.

Another country. No coinage she'd ever own.
Here was a vocabulary of smog and resentment,
glottal stops of surprise and unfinished sentences.
A pub caterwauled on almost every corner.

They'd chosen a painted capital, a circus of lights,
not this sooty England, this nation of billboards.
She'd shown the driver her purse. How much, she'd asked.
Take Courage, her eldest said. Make mine a Mackeson.

Sodium and neon and the more familiar moon
picked out their belongings, cases and parcels
that didn't belong. They were three in a bed,
listening to the strange language of buses.

The walls shook. A train mumbled underground.
Northern Line, Piccadilly. Change at St. Pancras.
Embankment. This way out. No way out.
She closed her eyes and tried to sleep.

        *   *

A teacher has clipped her eight year old
for choosing the airless cupboard to the playground.
She pushes past navy coats, ice runs by the toilets
and popped milk cartons to find out why.

Schubert's Trout is tinkling in the hall.
A class is in mid-chant. A new sound, this,
her black stilettos on the wooden floors.
There are pockmarks where others have been before.

He'd wanted the solace of paints,
blue like the sky, red like the earth.
But the earth is brown, his teacher says.
All this time and he doesn't forget.

Her eldest has been staring at her again.
Max Factor, she says. Rimmel and Fab. Get with it.
Her breath smells odd. She has a new way of standing.
A mannered slouch. Open the box. Take the money.

She counts. Rent on a Friday. Gas. Milk. Coal.
And she names. MacFisheries, Waltons, United Dairies.
Air mail, please. Par avion, please. Always say please.
One to Finsbury Park, please. The silver machine ratchets.

The conductor rings the bell. Twice to start,
once to stop. The white woman opposite her
is talking about him. Over here. Pink hands. Rubber lips.
Her big yellow hair is nodding. She has plastic eyelashes.

At the stop he helps with the shopping basket.
The big yellow head is still nodding as the bus pulls away.
There's a plane overhead. She's dazzled by its brilliance.
The man with the newsprint thumbs is watching her.

'My daughter says Fab and my son sees red earth.'
He smiles and shrugs. She buys flowers from Kapolka's.
Twelve early daffodils. It's nearly spring.
Soon they'll be growing everywhere.

On the Edge

An egg yolk eclipses itself on the ground.
Men go horizontal.

A dog turns into a howl
and women cover their heads.

Sparrows are caught mid-flight.
Feathers land on a car that won't start.

A girl runs to her mother's heart.
Four bullets bury themselves between their feet.

The mountains go crazy.
The trees spin like windmills.

Beyond this is roped off.

Americano

It's not like I want to be listening to Country
and Western in Starbucks or that I want to
study the glistening edges of a striped yellow
pencil. I'm trying to locate an open space. I was
almost getting to that place. But this one-two
one-two plonk, this slide of the next table's
German cadences over Japanese vowels, the
thunk of the barista's shoes on laminate
flooring. What I was thinking, what I was
hoping for was metal pins at the corners of a
board stretching the rat in a silent yawn. I was
trying to reach the formaldehyde stink of that
day, the museum shuffle of parents filing past,
the polish, the hush of old school labs. But
sugar spills and crumpled fivers, his arm across
her back almost touching, and girls laughing in
the corner. Someone fainted when the prefect
demonstrated an incision with a knife. She
removed both eyes. The biology teacher held
some calf-lungs and blew down the windpipe.
What I was hoping was not this. *It's not
democracy, sloping off to some summit then
saying fuck you we're doing it anyway.* A warm
spot with a rock, damn it. To sit on. Where the
words come like fishes and you winnow them
out. Not a West Bank bomb and unread papers.
Half a million, the UN said. Please. My
mother's hand. I'm leading the way. The sun's
filling the whole day. What I wanted. What any
of us wanted. On the wall. What we wrote,
what we learnt, what we hoped for. Projects,
artwork, next to the fire bell. What to do in the
event of an emergency.

If you're lucky you can fill a page easily in the
time it takes to drink their coffee.

Canyon

A winter afternoon. Look down between the perpendiculars
of Wright's Dental, Tex Mex Chicken. A woman's struggling
into the hypotenuse of rain, iglooed in her coat, dragging
a blue tartan shopping trolley behind her.

Heading west. Clip clop over the tracks.
Clip clop into the sullen waste of only one shop open.
(You can tell it by the lit up Coca Cola sign).
Clip clop into broken territory that used to be back to backs.

How the west was won: a high tensile fence,
two yellow lights screeling out of the cobalt gloom,
units to let, hard hats, maps, meeting room, board room.
I name this street Cody, Cassidy, Sundance.

Look up. You can see where each camera takes over
from the previous one. Security. Clip clop. Heading out.
It's all on film. The stranger becomes a silhouette.
Cue eerie whistling. Watch her grow small and disappear.

The rain turns to ice. Credits roll over the sudden night.
Cue music. Cut to Christmas trees and closing stores.
The hail is like dice pelleting the sides and doors.
Fade out when snow turns the big screen white.

Old Whiskey Mouth in the Drinking Shed

His fizzy eye wheels.
Break another can, he says.
The holy river bowls past.
He's a deep hole of a man,
soft, bomb-blessed.
Wine into music,
that's his smile.
Crack open another joke, he says.
Bad baby breathed.
Dribble sours his chin.
I leave him
amongst the sacking
and the few orange crates
he hasn't set fire to yet.
See you later, mate.
Not unless I see you first, he says.
And he doesn't.
When I come back
he's staring at the moon.
Clear stones on a warm night,
blue, sightless.
His mouth got stuck on a wheezing laugh.
That's how he looks.
Jack Daniels, mate.
I kiss the bottle to his lips
then wipe it clean,
as if my cuff
could take the taste
of him away,
could wipe the smell of death
from my own mouth.

MRI

A man floats down a river. Watch.
A man floats on his back down
a slow river, a calm river.

And listen. Birdsong.
There are no owls or crows.
Nothing ominous. These are

small birds, pleasant, reassuring
birds – sparrows and chaffinches.
Behind the man is a windmill.

We've taken great care with
the windmill. It has character.
It has grace and longevity.

It looks as though it might
still work. This is important,
to appear strong and dependable.

The man who is floating
can hear the birds. He can
hear the water cradling his body.

But he can't hear the poem.
The poem's outside the picture.
The poem's been chosen

for its soothing words.
The man is suspended
in a silver poem.

You're not supposed
to think about this.
You're not supposed

to remember how pens
and paperclips have been
sucked into the entry hole,

how years ago
an oxygen cylinder flew
off its stand and went ballistic,

or how a safety pin
you once swallowed might exit via
your unravelling belly-button.

Keep your mind on the man,
on the possibility of silent blades
slicing the air.

Forget
what happens next.
Forget what this might mean.

Capture a Sound

The cool ring of a woman's voice
over polished floors, the tiled interiors
of bistros, bars, roadside tabacs,

the clatter of plates, coins slapped down
on wood, on zinc, the flick of a lighter.

Laughter comes as thick
as coarse tobacco
and twice as dark.

The exact sound of summer.
No other like it.

Bikes slice past –
a collective thunk of gears changing down.

On Ventoux, the grimpeurs chat effortlessly,
basso profundo in pure air.

A bell rings out over Roussillon.
The dust gorges its clapped out throat.

Bees shroud the valley floor.
Lavender's a noisy business.

Some nights a cork squeals free and pops,
a tent's unzipped, zipped up, unzipped, zipped up.

Snake-pee hisses and wriggles in moonlight
or shrivels in secret behind the bushes.

You lie awake listening.
A litany. A chorus. Plainsong.

The telephone chirp of cigales.

An owl –
Hibou! Hibou!
A distant car.

Only the heat lightning has nothing to say.
It keeps up its silent babble all night.
It has an unmistakable talent for white.
A visual click that stays like a stuck needle.

Manatee

First there was thrumming darkness
then something round and bright,
my red blanket spinning away from me.
This is what I remember.
Her sad verruca eyes, crusty flowers,
crawling with sea lice, her snub-nosed prod,
yards and yards of grey-green silk.
She was round, like the back of a pebble,
a snib of plasticine turning in the warm silt.
How does a stone float? Like my mother.

And now I turn the same way,
repeat her endless circles.
The blades of boats open and close the sky.
The wound makes and unmakes itself.
I keep my belly down, my eyes fixed.
I look down, never rise above a certain point.

Death's Made You Bigger

It's given you an elongated back
and stretched you from side to side.

Moorhens shunt across you now.
Lily pads sprout impossible flowers.

Once, there was a heron staring
down the knife of its beak.

In summer you zigzag trees with light.
Wasps scribble around your shoulders.

Recently, there's been a door
behind your left ear.

You call it a portal, say it's something big,
like Star Trek.

Each day there are new curiosities
like willow dust and gadflies

and kingfishers
whose blue is too abrupt to understand.

Sift

A car park facing America. A black
western night where the rain came
down in spindles, so hard it bent
men double, lashed their coats
to their backs, forced rats from
flooded cellars. A Galway tinker
lies flat in his own stink. The bouzzies
laugh as they tie his feet together.
They watch him stumble and sway,
give up, throw both boots away.
A small brown dog chews them apart.
Up on the bluff, cattle low like rusty gates.
A local boy, all freckles and teeth,
kicks one boot down a hill, leaves
the other in shadow, collecting
dew, snow, blossom, silt. The doors
of the B&Bs, white sheets hanging
out to dry, fossil collectors, backpackers,
signs in Gaelic felt-tipped out
by some English wanker, a walker
with a gnarled stick and a packet
of sandwiches in a Londis carrier.
All these are possibilities. Tack-
tick, the biro licks out over the page.

The Cave

Before
was the impossibility of telling.

There were scenes in our heads
and no way of dancing them.

No songs
accompanied our daily rhythms.

A voice said yes or no
or let's go and that was all.

We never heard the wind play.
Play was not a word we understood.

The cave was in us all.
We couldn't see ourselves for lack of colour.

We couldn't see each other.
It was a kind of death.

Then one day a child pointed out
the texture of light and we stopped to listen.

Later, someone used a rock to describe their sorrow.
That's how it happened.

No one could stop it once it started.
No one wanted to.

Night Vision

It could be something small like a twig,
the way it snaps, or the way light nudges
a jar against its reflection in the window,
or how snow might fall in oblique threads
and tidy itself along the ledge one day,
only not steady, not nearly so steady,
more premeditated, the planned descent,
the way an absence of birdsong fills the evening.
Eyes swim like fish. The world is rolling
headlong and no one cares, so long
as it's loud and bright and forgetful.
It could be a switch. It could be traffic lights.
It's empty and lonely whatever starts it.

It's Not God

It's the smell of fallen apples and crushed nettles,
the way summer turns to rust overnight.

It's the platinum drift of clouds heaving themselves
onto fields of potatoes one afternoon,

or a feather pointing like an arrow down the road,
how birds balance in the wind,

how leaves press their photographic selves
into wet paving stones.

It's the silence of churches
and ink drying on the page,

the way people look when they shake hands,
tell the truth, hold the phone,

how a dog is when it's about to die.
It's about warnings and harvests.

Mostly, it's about you.

The Nobodies

We are the heads of children who leaned out of trains
when they were told not to, the non-stop laughs
that rolled on and on between jangling tracks,
the ones you could never shut up or make go away.

We tumble about like giant potatoes in an endless night.
Our bricked up lives are anonymous. You never see us
when you travel between one arch and another,
snatching at signals from your fading mobiles.

Hello, hello. We can hear you. Can you see us?
This one here looks like a battered biscuit tin,
his nose all caved in. And that one there's blonde and pretty.
Chocolate box pretty someone said. She never cared.

Her mouth stretched open at the rushing air
as the tunnel came and snatched her roar,
whisked her yellow hair to candyfloss
and spat her teeth to the screaming blackness.

Teeth. There are plenty here, though you'd never find them
in the little heaps of powdery smuts. We watch you
with your silvery laptops and your magazines
sealed in between shushing doors in the plastic warmth.

We're the ones who hurled everything at the sun,
the ones who never went to school again.
We are the heads of those who dared and never looked back.
We are the nobodies our parents tried to scare us with.

On Butler Avenue

Once, when I was lying in my aunt's breezeway,
the dead came to visit. What had they come for?
Why crowd around my bed? One by one they pressed
in through the doors. It was a family affair
going back centuries. Wall to wall, they were.
Like Ionesco's chairs. You could hardly move,
though I did, I turned to face them.
I lay for hours and watched.

How do you describe the dead - their legs,
their height and breadth, the way they slouch
or hold a cigarette, sit down, drink coffee?
The cadence of voices was different.
A biblical babble. Though I recognised some,
knew them by their names, had sat on their laps
when I was younger or swum with them,
I couldn't tell you who was who.
And there were some I'd never met.

They talked on through the night. A right old party.
I hardly slept. When day came, blue and sharp
against clapboard white, there was not an ornament
out of place, no rucked up rug, no sign to say
they'd been at all. My aunt was none the wiser.
The mailman came and went. We dined out,
did various things. I never mentioned it to her.
Just took the smell of polished wood with me,
the blood of blueberries, a nickel moon,
the feeling I'd come home again.

The Woman Upstairs

A word never finishes in the mouth - Ibo saying
i.m. K.C.

My grandmother declared war on her with a walking stick.
She banged on the ceilings and no Friday ever went past
without her saying something about the Sabbath oil.

When she saw her whisking something in a bowl
she called her Old Mother Pushpudding and the name stuck.

I did elaborate drawings of her underwear
pegged out over the bath. I gave her boils and scabs
and broken teeth. I drew her peeing herself.

Sometimes she watched us from her kitchen window.
Who didn't love the way my sister skipped and sang?

Hello Dolly Boots. She tried smiling and waving.
But we just stared or laughed and waited for her
to disappear behind the curtain again.

Once, she came down in a thunderstorm
and sat on a chair in the hall.

No one spoke. How fat and old and grey.
And us. How proud, how goy. She would have loved.
We could have. My sister said I wish you were dead.

And so she is. She tripped on a flex
and pulled the fire on top of herself.

She burnt like pork. Smelt like her rotten cooking,
my grandmother said. Except it wouldn't have been pork.
And it wouldn't have been the rubber of her corset, either.

My mother stayed with her till the ambulance came.
There was, I believe, a quiet undoing of words

Seven

It's the pitted moon and the stars and wondering if Hillary and Tenzing are women. It's not being able to breathe in the swimming baths, the four red fingermarks of a slap, the long worm trailing from a bucket. Seven is green. Lawnmowers, Vosene, the smell of crushed mint trodden underfoot, four-leafed clovers. Mostly, it's cabbage. And if it's a Wednesday sort of day, then it's standing at the top of the garden thinking this is me in my stripey T shirt and crumpled shorts, holding my arms out like Jesus. That's what seven is. Eating orange peel from the dustbin, lapping drainwater like a dog. Seven is pingpong looks over my head. Secret smiles, unsaid words. I say goodnightgodbless iloveyoumummy. She rocks my nightmares to the corner of the room. That's where it is. On TV. The White Heather Club and Robin Hall and Jimmy McGregor. Four Guinness bottles rattling in the basket on wheels. There are wolves down Hoop Lane. There's smoke from the crematorium. Letters from America arrive on shiny brown lino. There's beetroot on the table, Battenburg cake and cups of tea. The radio says Hilversum and Alloa. There's an orange thing in the back that comes on and goes off like a streetlight. It crackles and smells of dead insects. Here is the news. The white dot in the middle of the screen gets smaller and smaller and curiouser and curiouser aren't real words, everyone knows. I'm multiplied by seven and add one now. I shouldn't be thinking like this. But still nothing's changed. It's odd. The more I look, the more it stays the same.

Dust

Dust is a cast of thousands.
The ball of fluff behind your cooker is evidence.
Dissect it. Subject it to scrutiny.
You'll find previous lovers there,
cats, a mouse perhaps, the last tenant
and her snarling husband, an odd job man,
the plumber...

It takes seven years for the body to renew itself.
Our daily sheddings are emissaries,
proof we once existed.

When I was twelve, I witnessed a miracle -
rain the colour of rust on London's streets.
Sand, they said. All the way from the Sahara.
Grains from Mabrouk, Bir el Hadjaj, Arak, Tadjmout.
Like the Turin Shroud. A vision.
Pollens, sweat, and blood and hair.

If a cow can fly through air,
if tornados can rain down frogs,
then why not some remnant of arm or fingernail?

You cannot sweep away the past.
The carpet will always claim some fragment for its own.
Cleaning, any movement displaces things.
The past can never be consumed.
Your skin, your bone, your DNA -
you are who has lived before.

I'm vacuuming up my ancestors today,
laying down fresh deposits.
The dead are always with us:

Nana, Grampa, Gramma, Bert,

Great Aunt Blanche and Great Aunt Julia,
my father Robert, his brother Howard,
my cousin Louise and Thomas Heath Flood,
and Annie M. Winslow;
those bakers of bread and readers of Bibles,
Mary Oliver, Suzannah White,
swishing in black over rutted tracks,
keepers of poultry, brewers of ale,
makers of candles, menders of breeches,
child bearers, seafarers, strangers, begetters,
Edward, Josiah, Kenelm Winslow,
importers of cattle, importers of words,
looters of the Old World, governors of the New
and countless unknown First Nation people,
Mashpee, Nauset, Wonohaquaham, Namasket,
traders in fur and namers of moons,
grinders of corn and hunters of deer;
Louise and Mary and Charles Jaquith,
tillers of fields, choppers of wood,
Hannah, Deborah, Lidea Jaquith,
pressers of cheese, milkers of cows,
Abraham Jaquith, a bonded servant,
and unknown Franks, unknown Normans,
unknown Picts and unknown Celts,
forgers in bronze, shapers of iron,
builders of aqueducts, makers of tiles,
astronomers, weavers, growers of persimmons,
Minoans, Mycenaeans, and painters of rock,
inventors of time, makers of maps,
tellers of stories, trackers of comets,
inventors of words, inventors of fire;
African Eve, and back and back.
Two legs, four, no legs, gills.
Amoeba. Back.
And bang.